The Death of a Husband

Reflections for a Grieving Wife

Helen Reichert Lambin

ACTA

ASSISTING CHRISTIANS TO ACT

PUBLICATIONS

The Death of a Husband
Reflections for a Grieving Wife
by Helen Reichert Lambin

Edited by Patrice J. Tuohy

Cover Design by Tom A. Wright

Typesetting by Garrison Publications

Copyright © 1998 by Helen Reichert Lambin

Published by ACTA Publications
Assisting Christians To Act
4848 N. Clark Street
Chicago, IL. 60640
800-397-2282
www.actapublications.com

Library of Congress Catalog number: 97-77684

ISBN:978-0-87946-179-9

Printed in the United States of America

Year: 15 14 13 12 11

Printing: 10 9 8 7 6

Table of Contents

For Henry Joseph Lambin

in love, loss and gratitude

May your lifelong kindness be rewarded,
your love of learning never quite satisfied,
and your quiet wit bring a smile
to the most solemn of saints.

For Joe, Rosemary and Jeanne, who mourn him
as father and friend.

And for all those who are learning to live with
the death of a husband.

Introduction

The pages that follow were written in roughly chronological order, with a few exceptions. But they don't follow a neat, linear path from Profound Grief to Progressive Resolution. The reason, of course, is that grief itself does not follow a neat linear path from point A to point Z.

Grief is not a broad, straight highway sweeping like a ribbon across the plains, with road markers strategically placed so that you see not only where you're going but how far you've come—and how far you have to go.

Grief is a winding mountain road that circles and bends back upon itself, straightens out briefly, and then circles once again. There are very few road markers, and the destination is often completely hidden by the mountain itself. You can all too easily look back and see where you've come from. What's hard is to look ahead and see where you're going and know that you really have something waiting for you up the mountain.

Gertrude Stein once said of Oakland, California: "When you get there, there is no *there*, there." This is not the case with the destination of the winding road of grief. There is a *there*, there. This book is about that journey.

Never-ever Land

Careful. Here it comes again. Tick. Tick. Tick.
Creeping up. Lying in wait.
Pouncing when you least expect it.
Tick. Tick. Tick in the silence.
The sound of Never-ever Land.

No, not *Never-never Land*.

That was fantasy. And Wendy was a volunteer.
When she flew out the window with Peter and
Tinker Bell, nobody made her do it. In spite of
crocodiles and pirates, she had fun.

This is real. I am not a volunteer. And this is not,
by anyone's definition, fun. One day a wife, by
midnight a widow. Given a choice, I'd rather have
taken my chances with the pirates.

Welcome to Never-ever Land.

There is no signboard. There doesn't need to be. It
is enough to know that he will (or I will, or we will):

- never again come up the back steps, with his
  briefcase, raincoat and Greek fisherman's hat,
  while the dog waits by the gate.

- never again phone me at work, giving special meaning to a message light. (If I never answer the phone again, will they fire me?)
- never get to enjoy the retirement he earned and that I looked forward to spending with him.
- never again give that special smile turning up the corner of his mouth.
- never again prepare dinner so comfortably, knowing he'd be there to talk about the day's events and actually listen to my stories. (No matter how boring they were.)
- never again bring to bear his uncommon common sense.
- never again give him the benefit of mine.
- never again have that particular comfort and contentment of those quiet evenings at home, going our separate ways in the luxury of choice.
- never again experience the security of going to a party—or anywhere else—*together.*
- never again go to church and then to Sunday brunch *together.*
- never again plan a vacation *together.*
- never again wander the streets of a distant city holding hands.
- and never enjoy that surprise birthday celebration we were planning for summer, when we would make a point of telling him what he meant to us. (Instead, we said it at his funeral.)

In *Peter Pan* the menacing crocodile announced his coming by the tick, tick, tick of the clock he had swallowed. In Never-ever Land it's the clock itself that is so frightening, ticking away the silent hours while aching night follows aching day.

The dreaded *clock-o-dile*.

Measuring out the minutes and the hours and the days.

∞

Dawns

∞

It's not darkest just before the dawn. It's the dawns
themselves that are darkest—knowing there's another day to get through without you.

I used to love the dawn, in its quiet and freshness
and promise.

Dawns when the children were little, listening to the
birds outside the window and wishing time could
stand still for a few years.

Dawns when the children were grown, before the
alarm clock for work, relishing the interval of the
peace and stillness and the feeling that—whatever
else might be a worry—with you as the rock in my
life the world could be righted again.

Weekend dawns when I walked the dog early and
sang softly in the alley, for no other reason than
because I felt like singing.

The dawn in Quebec during our last summer together, when I woke you at 5:00 a.m. so we could
watch the sun over the St. Lawrence, pink and silver
and glowing, and it was only the beginning of another special vacation day.

And now all those precious dawns are stolen and the remaining ones vandalized, because death came for you in the night.

Somebody, can't you help me get my stolen dawns back?

⚭

The Radioactive Widow

⚭

Just when she began to be radioactive was difficult to say. In fact, she would not have even suspected she was, if it had not been for the lead shields she noticed people putting up after those first few weeks. People felt they needed to protect themselves from the waves she was emitting, because they were afraid of their force.

Some used the shield of *invisibility*. After the first few weeks they were rarely, if ever, seen or heard.

Others used the *deflecting* shield, which bounced the waves elsewhere. "You need to: see a therapist, find a group, look up some other widows, get a hobby, get out of yourself, talk to . . . someone else."

Still others used the *reflecting* shield, which simply wouldn't let any waves in by ignoring the treacherous opening "How are you?" and carefully pursuing other topics instead.

And finally there was *silver-lining* shield. "Well, it's in the natural course of things." "He died so suddenly. What a great way to go." "I know you feel bad, but everyone has problems."

No one used the shields to hurt her. But they were all so shiny and hard to look at that they brought tears to her eyes. She could understand why people were afraid of the waves. Maybe she would have used a shield, too, if *she* weren't the radioactive one.

Sometimes she wanted to shout: "If you think it feels bad from the outside, how do you think it feels from the inside?" But she couldn't get past the shields.

So she considered the various ways to deal with her situation.

Maybe she could go underground, where the waves would be muffled. Or perhaps she could go about in some kind of disguise, so no one would notice the waves. Or maybe . . . .

Fortunately, there were the special people. People who had no shields or who beat them into plowshares and helped her seek peace. Or those who laid down their shields and simply came within range of the waves to be with her.

As it turned out, the shields weren't necessary. She wasn't radioactive after all.

She was just grieving.

⚭

The Door

⚭

Why couldn't I have been the one to go first, my love? I know you didn't have any choice in the matter. But still . . . .

I used to say to you, conscious of the approaching years, "If you have any sense of decency, you'll let me go first."

"Isn't that rather selfish of you?" you would ask.

"Of course, it is," I said, selfishly. "But I still want to go first."

It didn't work out that way.

You would have handled it better, if I had gone first.

You could have played out some of your sorrows on the piano. Chopin would have worked well.

I don't play the piano.

You would have been that desirable creature—the extra, eligible man.

I am that problem person—the extra woman.

You could have taken refuge in one of your spontaneous, unexpected naps and escaped briefly into sleep.

You know I always had a touch of insomnia.

You, who always held doors open and stood back to let others through before you, went first through the one door I wish you would have held for me.

I keep pounding and crying, "Come back, come back." But the door stays closed.

I keep pounding and crying, "Can't you open it just a crack and let something through—a whisper, a dream, a few bars of Chopin heard in the silence of the night?" But the door stays closed.

Tell me, my courteous love, is there a closed door somewhere waiting for you to hold open for me so that we'll be together on the other side?

ༀ

Widow's Pique

ༀ

Hug me.
Try to understand me.
Listen to me as you'd want to be listened to.

Meet me for lunch, coffee, dinner.
But stop with the stiffen-your-spine exhortations
    already.
They don't help. They do hurt.

Hold my hand.
Lend me a book.
Don't pity me.

Weep with me.
Share your grief with me, and I'll weep with you.
But don't pretend that if you ignore it, it will go
    away.

If it hurts to hear about it,
think how it feels from the inside!

∽

Happy Memories to Forget

∽

"You have your happy memories.
May they comfort you in your sorrow."

Maybe sometime. But not now. It is all those happy
memories that make the present so unbearable.
They are the constant reminder of everything that
is lost.

Every happy memory is one more cry of pain,
echoing in the haunted present. Uninvited, unbidden, they follow from room to room, make themselves at home wherever they choose, interrupt
whenever they wish.

It's not that I want you forgotten by everyone—or
even by anyone. You deserve much better than that.
Let them speak of you for decades—your unassum-
ing goodness, your wisdom, your humor. You *should*
be remembered.

But if only you weren't remembered quite so well
by *me*.

Do I have to remember that quiet feeling of contentment, just knowing you were in the next room?

Do I have to remember what it felt like when one or both of us were worried, knowing that we could support and encourage each other—and find our way?

Do I have to remember our vacations, filled with a sense of adventure and magic that came from being shared?

Do I have to remember what it felt like just being together, all those days, all those years?

Couldn't I have just a little selective forgetting? Then maybe the hours wouldn't hurt so much.

Couldn't I remember how irritated we could sometimes be with each other, without remembering that even then your integrity and wisdom were something I could always trust?

Couldn't I remember you as someone I knew and liked, but not as my always best friend?

Is that asking for too much?

Then maybe I could get through the days and hours of now, instead of thinking of the way things were.

Then maybe I could enjoy an evening with family, lunch with a friend, a walk with the dog, a cup of tea on a leisurely Saturday morning.

If only *I* didn't remember so damn much!

⚭

Migration

⚭

Like flocks of birds in spring they come
Spreading their bright wings over those first days
of wake and funeral.
Twittering softly, soothingly the songs of comfort.
We'll be there for you.
We'll be there for you.

Like flocks of birds in autumn they depart
Spreading their dark wings against the grey sky
As they grow smaller, smaller in the distance.

The fruits of grief are too bitter to taste.
They will not stay.
They go to sip the nectar of wit and understanding
From those not shriveled by grief.

Up, up they go, their wings dark against the sky
Until they become pinpoints vanishing over the
horizon.

But here and there, nesting in the branches,
Here and there are the *rare birds,*
Gliding down to spread their bright wings
To sweeten the bitter fruit of grief with their
presence
To bring the fruit of comfort.

∞

Challenges And Conversations

∞

Why is it all right to pray at the tomb of Saint Francis of Assisi, who died 800 years ago?

But if I try to speak to you, it is denial?

Why is it accepted that millions flock to Lourdes for spiritual or physical healing, in the spirit of Mary and Bernadette?

But if I try to talk to you, it is an irrational way to ease my pain?

Why is it I belong to a faith based on a personal relationship with Jesus of Nazareth, who was executed 2,000 years ago?

Yet if I want the spirit of my spouse with me for the next decades, I am told I need to let go?

Why is it creative exploration if scientists seek radio signals from unknown life-forms in distant galaxies light-years away?

But if I seek the spirit of my spousal life-form from this galaxy, I am not getting on with my life?

Why is it that *doubt* has such *conviction*?

Why is it that *conviction* is so vulnerable to *doubt*?

∞

Lucky

∞

A good way to go. So quickly. He was so lucky!
    some say.
As though he won some marvelous,
    unexpected prize.

Collapsing in the morning
Healthy the day before
Dying in one day
As he fought to live.

He was so lucky!

Yes, I understand what is intended.
Prolonged illness casts a long shadow of sorrow.
Who would not spare those they love?

But lucky?

Luck was not obvious when he collapsed that
    ordinary morning as we were talking.
Nor when he struggled to his knees
Insisting he would walk to the hospital
Fearing, perhaps, the ambulance that would
    take him on his last ride.

Luck was not obvious when the silent killer
        in his arteries burst
Unseen, unfelt until that moment it burst
Bleeding into that kind heart,
Even while I spoke of recovery.

Luck was not obvious as he wrestled for life,
        impatient at his weakness.
Nor when I left the hospital, planning to return
        tomorrow,
Not knowing tomorrow would be forever changed.

So tell me things work out in odd ways.
I may find comfort in that.
Tell me he might have preferred to go as he did
        before losing himself to himself.
I may agree with you.
Tell me your grief, and I will grieve with you.

But lucky?

He didn't win the lottery.
He died.

Forgiveness

For every unkind word I ever said to you,
      forgive me.
I would eat them word by word now if I could.

For anything I ever did to hurt you, forgive me.
I would do it all over and do it right, if I could.

And for anything that you'd undo, forgive yourself.
It really doesn't add up to much in all those years.

Except, I might add, for all your papers and books.
I asked you to sort through them—
The ones we're going through now week by week.
Don't you wish you'd done it, after all?

I know, it's not fair of me to bring it up when
      you can't bring up my flaws.
Anyway, you were never one to hold a grudge.

But I'll tell you something learned in the silence.
It's scant compensation for your absence
      to have the last word.

Balloons in the Wind

⚭

I have to admit I didn't pray *for* you, at first. It seemed to me that if your wife could say, "Truly this was a good man," that God could say no less. Particularly since God could not possibly be as judgmental as I.

If anyone needed prayers, it was your family, as we learned to live in a world without you.

But now, I've changed my mind. Not about your kindness and integrity. Nor about God's. But maybe you'd like our prayers, maybe you need our prayers, as *you* learn to live a new way in a new world.

So, sometimes I pray for you, and sometimes I pray *to* you.

Do you hear me calling. Are you listening? I can't be sure.

Of course, I couldn't always be sure before, either. You were so good at not making it obvious if you weren't listening. And maybe, after all, you're glad to hear from us, too.

There they go, then, the prayers ascending like silvery balloons, up over the treetops, into the clouds. And whatever prayers you don't need, off they drift, wind-borne, blown off course where needed by the breath of the Spirit.

Wolf Cry

Grief is a gaunt grey wolf.

Howling at a winter moon.
    Listening
    Listening
    Listening
For the echoing call from the distant hills.
The absent voice of her mate.

Being jostled to the edge of the pack.
    Running
    Running
    Running
To avoid being left behind.
A lone wolf lost in her memories.

Awakening to the sleeping silence of the den.
    Waiting
    Waiting
    Waiting
For his shadow on the snow.
Waking to remember there can be no shadow.

Grief is a gaunt grey wolf.

∞

Superwidow

∞

What do you mean, get on with my life?
What do you think I'm doing?

Walk the dog.
Go to work.
Clean the refrigerator.
Cry.

Write checks for the bills.
Call a friend.
Get names of electrician, carpenter, plumber.
Find out how to turn off the furnace.
Find a bereavement group.
Write a thank-you note.
Rehash the good old days with the kids.
Get depressed.

Do the laundry.
Watch a video.
Fill out forms.
File papers.
Survive.

Go to bed.
Wake up early.
Lie awake.
Worry.

Wish it were last year.
Read a book.
Make a budget.
Look into a used car.
Do what has to be done.

Superwidow.

Then why do I feel so scared and shaky and sad?
Why do I just want to crawl in a hole and hibernate
       for a decade or two?
Okay, so maybe not Superwidow.
But getting through another day.
Doing what has to be done.
More or less.
Hanging in there day by day.
More or less.

They say, you've gotta do what you've gotta do.
But nobody can say I've gotta like it.

∞

Possibility

∞

Yesterday was a better day. For a brief time, I felt somewhat like the old Me. Maybe a small "somewhat." But at least the Me was vaguely familiar, instead of this sad stranger living in my skin.

It didn't last, of course. By this morning the feeling of "better" had gone to the Limbo of the Heart where the shades of dead feelings hang about, trying to reshape themselves.

But still, for those few hours, it gave a glimpse of the possibility that there could be other days to come that would be better, other days where I would again feel somewhat like Me.

∞

The Growing Season

∞

It was a great growing season while it lasted.
Being solidly rooted in you.
And you solidly rooted in me.

It kept me from being fragmented
      by the occasional high wind.
It helped me spring back, resilient
      when I was flattened by sudden storms.

It gave me the chance to grow and flourish—
      to store up the sunlight.
And to reach deep into the earth for moisture
      during the occasional dry spell.

To bring forth some splendid new shoots
      for the family tree.
Each one different.
Each one beautiful in shape and shadings
      life and color.

Yes, it was a fine growing season while it lasted,
      before the killing frost.

But now how do I put down roots to get me
      through the winter?
Will there be another growing season,
      without you?
Will I come out strong enough to weather the
      conditions to come?

Are our roots still intertwined?
Invisible?
Indivisible?

What will I grow into?
What will I be?
Now that it is *I* not *we*.

∞

Could You Not Spare One Hour?

∞

If only I knew it wouldn't be so long before I saw him again, Lord, I could get through this.

If only I knew that I could see him once a year for a week, I could handle being a widow. Not easily. But it would be better than the indefinite wait.

There would still be the dark days. But at least there would be a light in this long tunnel of grief.

If only I could be with him . . .

- for a week, once a year. Just one week out of 52. Is that asking too much?

- all right, so maybe even just for a day, one day out of 365. Surely you could spare one day out of an eternity of them?

- Or even an hour a year. One hour out of 8,760. Surely that is not unreasonable, Lord?

I'd promise not to ask him any questions that would disclose trade secrets. Like . . .

- What do you do where you are now? Are there really choirs of angels? What is the eternal He (or She) like?

- Who is there with you? Who is not?

- What is going to happen tomorrow? Will the children have happy lives?

- How did it all begin? Did it really start with a Big Bang?

- What is the answer to the problem of suffering?

- Will the stock market go up or down?

- How does it feel in transition? Have you spoken with Mother and Dad? Were the dogs and cats there to greet you?

- When do I finally join you? How will it happen? Should I worry about making it at all?

Even if I asked, he wouldn't answer, Lord. You know how careful he was about keeping confidences.

And if there's any question, I'll gladly sign whatever contract you wish. "The party of the second part (that's me) agrees not to ask any questions about what goes on *After*. And the party of the first part (that's You) agrees that X can spend one hour each year with his wife."

If it's a problem, he and I don't even need to talk. Just sitting holding hands would be fine, and to see him smile once again. Could the children be there, too, for maybe 15 minutes? Or am I pushing my luck?

Yes, I realize that he is in a more advanced state now, one I cannot even begin to comprehend. So maybe if we *did* talk, it would be hard for me to understand him. But that's okay, too. Anyway, maybe you could temporarily block out or delete the advanced knowledge. I would be perfectly happy to see him just the way he was.

I know, Lord, it would mean my having to let him go again, until the next time. And that would never be easy. No matter how many times I do it. But it would also mean being able to say hello again the next time, instead of waiting it out along the long corridor of years.

I know, Lord, his spirit is with me now. And don't get me wrong. I'm very grateful for that.

But still, would it be asking too much to ask for more? Just that one hour out of so many?

Would it be so difficult? For you who raised the mountains from the sea and scattered the stars and envisioned giraffes and butterflies?

Could you not let me have just one week, one day, one hour? To get me through until I join You and all the others and the hour moves out of time?

꩜

The Family Dog

꩜

What are you like now that you are in an advanced
state? Would I recognize you?

How would we communicate, if we sat down for a
talk? Would I still understand you? Or would it be like
holding a conversation with the family dog?

She likes to go for a walk with me and sit by my side,
even if we can't discuss books or world affairs, or
share the newspaper, or plan a vacation together,
although maybe she'd like to go, too.

If I sat down to tell her about my day and what's
happening with the family, maybe what she would
hear is:

- good dog
- stop that
- din din
- who's a pretty girl?
- get out of the garbage
- walkies
- want a cookie?
- here's a hug.

And maybe what I would hear and understand from you is only a fraction of what you have to tell me. But still, right now I'd gladly settle for:

- good human
- keep away from the garbage
- who's a pretty person?
- here's a hug.

∞

How Could You?

∞

How could you have accumulated those thousands of books? Never disposing of one!

- books read long ago
- books to read someday
- books stacked on shelving
- books piled in corners
- books stuffed under furniture
- books gathering dust
- books I have to sort through now that you're gone
- every book a reminder of you.

How could you have kept every piece of mail you every received? Every note you ever jotted down?

- assembly instructions for bicycles long gone
- warranties for appliances worn out
- cancelled checks from cancelled decades
- motel receipts from long-ago vacations
- ideas for articles you'd write someday
- reflections on ideas

- file after file of ideas
- papers I have to sort through now that you're gone
- every piece of paper a reminder of you.

Didn't I tell you to sort through all this stuff?
Didn't I tell you
Again and again and again?

My back aches.
My shoulders aches.
My heart aches.

All those years I wanted to have *you*,
Without your *clutter*.

And now look what happened.

⚭

Between Him and Me

⚭

If you're listening, Lord,
To my how-could-yous,
Don't get involved.
This is between him and me.

I wouldn't want him penalized
Or privileges withdrawn
Or his early eternity tainted in any way.

He was a good man, a good father, a good husband,
A good companion, a good friend.
If the worst you can say about someone is that he's
        a pack rat,
It says a lot about the good.

So, yes, it's a hell of a mess to clean up,
If you'll pardon the expression.
But maybe it's part of the price
For the good parts of all those years.

So, remember, Lord, if you're listening,
It's between him and me.
I wouldn't want him to feel guilty
As he explores his new world of love and learning
Just because I'm caught in clutter on Norwood
        Street.

Well, maybe just a *little* guilty.

Not enough to tarnish his happiness,
You understand.
Never that.

But maybe just a little twinge of guilt now and then,
As he explores your boundless, clutter-free frontiers.

⚭

The Great Pretender

⚭

"Oh yes, I'm the Great Pretender . . . ."
                                        —the Platters

I can get through today.
I'll just pretend that you went to a concert after work.
Popcorn, candy and TV this evening.
And no dinner to cook.

I can get through this week.
I'll just pretend that you are visiting your sister in
        St. Louis.
You'll be back in Chicago in no time.
But do drive carefully.
And it would be nice if you'd call home just to talk.

I can get through this month, I guess.
I'll just pretend that you are out of town for some
        kind of extended training.
But I wish you had fixed the garage door lock
        before you left.
And it's just not the same without you.
I wish you'd drop me some postcards—
And call home now and then just to talk.

I can even get through this year without you,
        I suppose.
People did it during the war.

I can pretend you are assigned to some safe
        but secret mission.

But I wish we had talked about important details
        before you left.
And the days are getting long without you.
Your children, grown up or not, miss you.
Your granddaughter is forgetting your name.
The dog waits every night by the gate.
And I'm ready to go out and wait with the dog.

This day, this week, this month, this year.
I can handle it. It's not forever, after all.

But how am I going to handle 10, 20 or 30 years?
With no calls, cards, letters, visits.
Only the weight of all those years,
        with all those weeks and hours
        pressing in like rocks,
        building a prison of days.

I can't go on being the Great Pretender.
If I'm to go on at all.

It's either *belief* or *disbelief,*
But no *pretend.*

I choose belief.
Belief that you have, in fact,
        emigrated to another land.
Belief that you will wait for me to arrive someday
        on that other shore.

Getting Through

I'm eating a little better now.
Those first weeks after you were gone all I could eat
    were soup and soft things
And I lost the weight I had thought of losing
    for a year.
And resented it.
It seemed such a waste—who was there
    to admire me?

I am sleeping a little better now.
Those first months after you were gone,
    I lay in the darkness
And waited for daylight
So I could get up and walk the dog
    and begin another day
That I wondered how I'd ever get through.

It's not good.
At least not good in the way it used to be.
But at least it's not, at all moments, as bad as it was.
It's not happiness.
At least not happiness in the way it was before.
But at least now and then the misery ebbs.

Maybe that's because of a gradually growing
        conviction that what I believed in all
        those years—
Until you died and I suddenly believed in nothing—
        is true:
That there is life beyond life, and that you *are*
        just fine.
Still living, loving, learning, in a state I cannot
        describe or even imagine.

Maybe in part because of a gradually growing sense
        of your continuing presence and love.
Not the visible, tangible presence I so long for
        and so miss.
Not a domesticated specter that conveniently
        materializes, takes shape and speaks in words.
Although, oh, it would be nice if you would!

The Children

∞

Your children consider themselves half-orphans.
Even if they are young adults now.
Even if they are my children, too.

They grieve together as a family.
But each grieves a separate grief.

One sees in the rose bush all the summers you
        were there trimming it—the symbol of
        your presence.

One looks for your car in the expressway rush hour,
        going north as you went south—the symbol of
        coming home.

One would save every piece of paper you jotted an
        idea on—a paper fence to keep the past from
        escaping.

Together they remember their childhood,
        their father, their bonds.
Going their separate ways to learn
        that grief binds us together.
But grief is lived alone.

I tell them I feel half-orphaned, likewise.
But I don't know whether they believe me.
Even as they try to do things for me
        they think should be done.

But a mother-orphan?
I'm supposed to be the official grown-up now.

Every house should have one.
But how did it get to be me?

∞

Florence

∞

How can you be happy knowing we are so unhappy without you?

Not that I begrudge it. This is one time when misery does *not* love company! If I didn't think you were happy, that would be the most miserable thing of all.

But still, it's hard to understand your being happy—you who were always so tenderhearted, you who felt so sorry for the dog when we brought her home in a cast, you who were so empathetic. If it were the other way around, could I be happy when you were not?

I've thought about it a lot, and still haven't come up with any answers. Just an analogy.

It's like you've arrived early in Florence, Italy, while my flight has been delayed for some time. (And still longer, I hope, the arrival of the rest of the family!)

So there you are, in some wonderful place, running into people you knew and loved and haven't seen for years.

Meanwhile, here I am, sad and sulky among my suitcases, because you caught that earlier flight.

Then along comes a tour guide and gives you a choice. Would you like to wait in Florence for the others to arrive? Or would you prefer to rejoin them in Gary, Indiana?

I know what I might say. Thanks, but I'll wait here.

So you may as well enjoy yourself. And time probably seems much different where you are. For all I know, it's a matter of days to you.

Your sense of time was different, even here. For 30 years I nagged you about being late. And now the one thing—*the one thing*—I wanted you to take plenty of time in doing, you have to rush!

So, *arrivederci* for now, *caro*. See you in Florence when my flight is called.

∞

Why?

∞

Lord, I know you have reason for what you do.
At least, that's what they tell me.

So, tell me, Lord, *why?*

Why did you have to take this good man *now*?
A good husband.
A good father.
Good at his daily job.
A man who brought good to others.

Don't you understand how much we need him?
His wife.
His children.
Even the family dog.

So, I ask you, Lord, *why?*
Why, if you were going to call someone to you,
        did it have to be *him?*
Don't we need all the good people we can find
        around here?
Are they so expendable?
Is there such an oversupply?

Look around you, Lord, weren't there other
        choices?
Those who leave waves of misery in their wakes.
Infamous woe-makers and more anonymous ones.
You don't need a list.

They say that when God calls, you answer.
Well, I guess so.

But still, I ask you, *why?*
Why now?
Why him?
Why *me?*

Life Sentence

What did I do?
How did I get here?

I don't remember a trial.
Still less do I remember pleading guilty.
Yet here I am.
Serving a life sentence in this prison of grief.

I demand to see my lawyer.
Don't I get at least one phone call?

And let it be to my husband.
If he were here,
He could get me out of this place.

Don't I have the right of appeal?
What happened to my constitutional rights—
Life, liberty and the pursuit of happiness?
Do I get credit for good behavior?
What are the possibilities for parole?

One day I was just an ordinary person,
Living an ordinary life.
A *happy,* ordinary life.
The next day, here I am.

I don't belong here, I tell you.
There must be some mistake.

Well, listen to me, Your Honor.
And don't hold me in contempt.
Don't think I'm going to take this quietly.
I'm not. I can't!

The work assignments are getting to me.
So much to do without him.
So different from doing things with him.

From the outside it may not look like a prison.
From the outside it looks like everywhere else.
No barbed-wire topped walls.
No guard towers to prevent escape.

They aren't needed. The walls stretch.
When you move, they move,
Always keeping you inside.

Sometimes even from the inside you get
        confused.
And hurl yourself blindly against the walls,
But the walls stand.

As for the inmates, you meet the nicest people.
Including your family. Your friends.
And there are the prison visitors who come
        to help hold your pain.
But it's still a prison.

Hello, out there . . .
Is anyone listening?

∞

Noah's Ark

∞

Two by two they travel around the ark.

Old and young.
Black and white.
With children.
Without children.

Couples.

Two by two they make their way.

Saturday shopping in the supermarket.
Talking over coffee in a restaurant.
Pushing a stroller through the park.
Shared excitement waiting at the airport.
Exchanging glances at a party.

Couples.

It's the way to travel aboard the ark.

Don't be envious, instant experts tell us,
When you see other couples and wish it
        were you.

Don't be envious, you tell yourself firmly,
When you see other couples and remember
        when it was you.

Do I begrudge them having what I once had?
How could I?
Love should be spread around.

Do I resent their time together?
How could I?
This sadness is the price I pay now for then.

Do I ever feel envy, when I see them?

Couples, couples, couples,
Casually making their way through the ark.
Taking for granted what I now cherish.

Do I ever feel envious?

Damn right I do.

Tree Of Knowledge

The rabbi said it:
The priest said it:

"At a time like this
You find out who your friends are."

The rabbi said it:
The priest said it:

"At a time like this—unfortunately—
You also find out who they are not."

∞

Pronouns

∞

Then:

We

Our

Ourselves

Ours

Us.

Now:

I

My

Myself

Mine

Me.

Pronouns hurt.

The Invisible Visible Woman: Part I

There are innumerable secondary losses accompanying the death of a husband. Losses you begin to become aware of after the first shock of *the* loss wears off. One of these secondary losses, according to various experts in the field, is loss of status. The widow is somehow seen as diminished from what she was as a wife. That's bad enough. But what is worse is that widows tend to accept this view of ourselves. And thus we experience not only loss of status but of self-esteem.

It is as though math rules no longer hold. Two minus one does not leave one. It leaves something less than one—perhaps a half-person—or, rather, a semi-visible one. This happens in the media, as in life. Consider television: How many widows do you find in recurring roles? And when they do appear, what are their characters like?

A few years back there was a successful sitcom about four mature women sharing a home. Three were widows, one divorced. The divorced woman was presented as strong, witty, and a leader. Of the three widows, one was an attractive nymphomaniac; one sweet, kind and dense; and the oldest of the trio was generally gaga. It made for entertaining television. It did not make for widowed self-esteem.

Yet suddenly becoming a widow is a time when self-esteem is badly needed. Not in the sense of pseudo self-esteem—self-illusion—in which we can't acknowledge our flaws. We weren't perfect before we were widowed. Why would we suddenly become so overnight? But self-esteem in the sense that the widow is a person with a role and an identity, with hopes and possibilities and problems—just like other people.

We have our self-esteem when we are not less than one, even though we are no longer half of two.

The Invisible Visible Woman: Part II

Widows in Scripture

The second-class role of women in the centuries of the biblical era has been pointed out by writers from cultural anthropologists to scripture scholars. It would be difficult to argue that it wasn't so. But at the same time there are women, and among them widows, who do play a significant role in scripture stories.

Ruth and Naomi: The story of Ruth is the story of a journey with far-reaching results. When Ruth, a young Moabite woman, is widowed, she accompanies her mother-in-law, Naomi—also a widow—to Naomi's homeland of Judah. Their bond of kinship and fidelity is expressed notably in Ruth's lines: "Wherever you go I will go. . . . Your people shall be my people, and your God my God."

While working in the fields in Judah, Ruth meets and, with some assistance from Naomi, eventually marries the landowner Boaz, a kinsman to Naomi. It is the beginning of a new life for Ruth. But it is also part of a larger story. Ruth, with Boaz, becomes one of the ancestors of Jesus, according to the genealogy in the Gospel of Matthew. And Naomi, whose faith survived the loss of her husband and sons, contributes to the events leading to the coming of the Messiah. *(The Book of Ruth)*

Bathsheba: Bathsheba is the beautiful bather whom King David sees from the roof of his palace. As the story of David and Bathsheba begins, Bathsheba is not a widow. She is the wife of Uriah the Hittite, a soldier in David's army. David covets Bathsheba and seduces her, and when she becomes pregnant David plots to have Uriah sent to the battlefront, where he is killed. David has made Bathsheba a widow and then marries her. For what he has done, there are heartbreaking consequences. The first son of David and Bathsheba dies, and while in mourning David is called to repentance by the prophet, Nathan. Bathsheba later bears David another son, named Solomon. With Nathan's counsel and Bathsheba's maneuverings, Solomon eventually succeeds David as king, and Bathsheba becomes Queen Mother.

In Matthew's genealogy, Solomon is part of the Davidic line of succession leading to Jesus. Bathsheba, too, as his mother, is part of the line of succession. She is listed by Matthew as "the wife of Uriah," her first husband. Like Ruth and Naomi before her, the widowed Bathsheba played a role in events reaching far beyond her life. *(2 Sam. 11:2–1 Kings 1:12)*

The Poor Widow and the Prophet: The anonymous widow in the brief miracle story in Second Kings is not a queen-to-be and is far from a palace. She is so poor and debt-ridden that her creditors are threatening to sell her two sons into slavery. The only thing she has in her house is a jar of oil. Desperate, she approaches the prophet Elisha for help, reminding him of her faithfulness to the Lord. Elisha counsels her to borrow as many empty vessels as possible from the neighbors and begin pouring the oil from her jar into them. She and her children do so, without questioning how it will work. The oil from that single jar flows so plentifully that every vessel they borrow is filled. Elisha then tells her to sell the oil and pay her debts, and then she and her children can live on the rest. We hear no more about her. Just an anonymous woman, widow and mother, driven to the brink of desperation, sustained by faith. *(2 Kings 4:1-7)*

Anna: Anna was not aided by a prophet. Anna was a prophet. The Gospel of Luke does not tell us much about her—just a tantalizing glimpse. Widowed after seven years of marriage, Anna spent her days and nights at the Temple in prayer and fasting. Then, at the age of 84, came the extraordinary event to which those years were leading. She encountered the infant Jesus. Anna the prophet recognizes the encounter for what it was—the presentation of the Messiah—and "immediately she began to praise God and speak about the child to all who were looking for the redemption of Jerusalem." What were those long years like? Were they often lonely, sometimes hard, filled with worry, regrets, "if onlys"? Luke does not say. We only learn that her long road led to the Lord. *(Luke 2)*

The generous widow: The Gospel of Luke tells us another brief story of another anonymous widow. It is near the end of Jesus' ministry, and he is teaching in the Temple in Jerusalem. At the Temple he sees the wealthy putting their gifts into the Temple treasury; he also sees an impoverished widow putting in two copper coins. (The small copper coin was referred to as a *mite* in earlier translations—hence, the phrase "the widow's mite.") Jesus holds up her actions as a lesson in generosity. The well-to-do have contributed out of their abundance. She has contributed out of her poverty and need. *(Luke 21:2)*

Mary: Scripture does not specify that Mary, the Mother of Jesus, is a widow, but it suggests it. After she and Joseph find Jesus at the Temple in the Gospel of Luke, neither the gospels nor the epistles refer to Joseph again. Since his fidelity and responsibility earlier is amply demonstrated, it would appear that he died before Jesus began his public life. Mary is alone at times of joy and sorrow. She is the initiator of the miracle at the wedding feast at Cana. She stands at the foot of the cross when Jesus has been deserted by most of the disciples. She is told that John is now to act as her son. When the disciples gather to pray before Pentecost, Mary and several other women are present when the Spirit descends in wind and fire. After the descent of the Spirit in Acts, Luke, who speaks the most of Mary, does not refer to her again. What did she do afterward? She would have been approximately 50—not the young girl of the "let it be done unto me" but a mature woman who had experienced the best and worst life has to offer—a woman who ultimately would be recognized as the Mother of God.

The stories of Ruth, Naomi, Bathsheba, the anonymous widows, Anna and Mary were all considered important enough to be passed on by oral tradition before they were finally committed to the written word.

Being a widow is a role one rarely chooses. It is a role thrust upon us. But it still needs to be played out as well as possible. As with all widows before us, where our destiny calls us, we must go.

The Unset Clock
and the Wound-up Dog

Once upon a time there was a new widow named Soledad, who lived in an old house in a big city, along with her middle daughter, a dog and three cats. She had not been a widow for very long— three weeks. And she did not think she was very good at it.

Every night she paced the floor and said to her departed husband: "Oh, if only you were here. However am I going to live without you?"

But there was no answer.

And every day she paced the floor and said: "If only I knew that you were all right, that you were as happy as you deserve to be, I could live with this. Not easily. But I could."

But there was no answer.

It was not that she was unsure what type of place he deserved. If a wife can say, "Here was a deserving man," how could God, who didn't share a house with him, say less?

But there was a nagging question creeping in at the back of her mind: What if, after all, there *isn't* a place. What if he's just . . . extinguished?

It wasn't that she expected a major miracle or high drama, such as a thundering voice from the heavens saying "He's fine!" or a letter embossed in gold leaf with her husband's signature witnessed by one of the better-known saints and delivered by an angel— although that would be nice.

All she wanted was a small, quiet sign, a hint—subtle and delicate—that, however much they were hurting without him, *he* was just fine.

But there was no sign—small, quiet or otherwise.

Then, one Saturday evening when her daughter was at work and she was alone, she said to the walls, "Oh, if only you were here. However am I going to live without you?"

But there was no answer.

"If only I knew that you were all right," she said to the windows. "That you were as happy as you deserve to be, I could live with this."

But there was no answer.

She turned back her bed and took a bath and wished she could turn back time and crawl into a nice warm year—like the year before. As she plodded down the hall, she saw a tail disappear around the corner and remembered she had forgotten to take the dog out.

When her husband was alive, he took care of this night walk.

It had become a stand-up routine. Every night he would set his alarm clock for 10:15 p.m. to remind himself to take the dog out, but almost every night he would fall asleep and not hear the alarm. So the widow, who was not then a widow, would walk into the room where he was napping and say, "Your alarm clock is going off. Why do you set it if you don't hear it?"

And he would say, "Oh, it is. I didn't hear it."

Then she would say, "Are you going to take the dog out?"

And he would say, "Why do you ask? Don't I always?"

And she would say, "Yes."

But now there was no one to take the dog out. And no one to nag about it. "Oh, if you were here, oh, if only you were here," she said, as she had said so many times before in the last three weeks.

But this time there was an answer. Maybe.

Because suddenly, into the silence, she heard the sound of an alarm clock going off in the empty room down the hall. A clock that should have been silent, because no one had set the clock for weeks. No one ever did set that clock except her husband. Could it have fallen over? But that would turn the alarm *off*, not *on*—for the clock was one of those inexpensive electric clocks with a little plunger that had to be pulled *out* to set the alarm—the alarm that was ringing now in an empty room.

She looked at her watch. It was 10:15 p.m. "Oh, God," she said. "Oh, my God," and it was not irreverence, yet not quite a prayer. It was a statement of awe in the face of the inexplicable.

With the sound of the alarm bell ringing in her ears and in her soul she went down the hall to the empty room and pushed the plunger in, to turn off the alarm. Then she went to the kitchen to phone one of her daughters to tell her about the clock—and to let the dog out.

While dialing, she reminded herself to be sure to let the dog in, for the night was chilly and the dog would never bark to be let in. She would just sit there, shivering in silence outside the back door—unless someone came into the house while she was outside. Only then would she bark to be let in.

But not this night. Suddenly, in the middle of the phone conversation, the dog began barking to be let in. Which was much to the surprise of the widow, because no one had come into the house.

She put down the phone, watching the dog. The dog ran first to the front door, looking bewildered. Then, barking joyously, tail wagging, the dog ran upstairs toward the empty room.

What happened that night as the widow was saying, yet again, "Oh, if only you were here"?

What do *you* think?

Later, after she held it in her heart for a while, the widow told the story of the clock and the dog to various friends.

Some said, in surprise, "What an odd, wonderful thing."

Some shyly told stories of their own odd and wonderful things.

And the widow smiled, listening and remembering.

And some said, embarrassed. "Well, yes, but I think there's probably some simple explanation."

But the widow just smiled, listening and remembering.

Could they explain it? Maybe.

But maybe not. Because *they* weren't there when the alarm clock rang in the three-week silence and the dog barked in joyous greeting on the empty stairs.

#*%@&!

It is something of a shock in these anything-goes days, when almost anything can and is said anywhere, that there remains an expression so vulgar and profane as to require the symbols of an expletive deleted. But that is how it is with death. Death has replaced personal and sexual activity as an inappropriate topic. It has become something not to be spoken of in polite company—outside of the formal ritual of wake and funeral.

It is as though the deceased has somehow disgraced himself and his family by dying, and the kindest thing to do is tactfully ignore the whole thing. Death becomes the ultimate obscenity, a kind of five-letter four-letter word.

In some cases this happens because of the best of intentions. People don't know what to say and therefore don't. In other cases, perhaps, it is because people don't want to deal with the unpleasantness. "You need to get on with your life now" means "I want to get on with mine." It is human nature to want things to return to normal in our lives. But it still hurts the person with no *normal* to return *to*.

Whatever the response, whether kindness and empathy or dismissal and change of subject, death should not be an unmentionable. It is as mysterious as it is inevitable. It carries with it a whole cluster of secondary experiences and changes. It can be expected or unexpected; natural or accidental; peaceful or violent. It can be a sudden thunderbolt or a gentle breeze of relief.

Whatever the events, the word *death* is not an obscenity. It speaks of many things—of tragedy and transition, of love and loss and longing.

But when a widow really feels misunderstood and abandoned or tired of coping with the insensitivity of others, she is allowed to say silently to herself: #*%@&!

Party

Party.
Deciding whether to go.
Without you.
Deciding what to wear.
Does it matter?
Who there could penetrate my disguise as you
      could?
Seeing behind the mask of years the young woman
      you married.

"How do I look?" I'd ask you.
It isn't even so much the answer I miss now.
It's the being able to ask.
"Can't you hurry?" I would ask.
Lines spoken how many dozens of times?
But if I knew you were going to be with me tonight,
      even for a moment.
Oh, how patiently and silently I could wait!

Party.
I go alone.
"Hi, how are you?"
"Okay, yes, hanging in."
"No, nothing new."
How am I? Who am I?
Half of something that isn't here.

Running out of chitchat.
Smile getting frayed at the edges.
How did I used to do this?
As a wife!
Arriving together, we'd move around separately.
But never alone.
Even if you weren't there, you were always there.
Waiting at home. Or arriving late. Coming to meet
    me.
Everyone glad to see you.
What a sensation you'd cause if you showed up now!

"It's getting late." I'd say. *"When do you want to
    leave?"*
"What's your hurry," you'd answer. *"We just got
    here."*
If only you were here with me now, I'd stay till dawn,
    I promise.
I'd stay for days. I'd stay till they threw us out.

Maybe I can leave quietly.
Sneak into the kitchen and call a cab.
It's full of people.
Think of something else.
Maybe I can cadge a ride with someone who's
    leaving early.
Good idea. Ask. Casual. Unobtrusive. No fuss.
The host, trying to be helpful, stops a departing
    guest.
"Can you give her a ride?" he asks them.
"No," they reply regretfully, "We have a
    carful already."
No problem, I say, smiling as expected.

Finally, someone is going my way.
"Thanks. It's been a lovely evening.
It was so nice of you to ask me."
And it was nice. It really was.
Maybe what I really need now is to be invited.
Without necessarily actually having to go.
An absent, but welcome, recluse.

Arriving home.
Friends waiting while I unlock the door.
Turn and wave. Lighthearted. Thanks.
Home.
Take off coat.
Take off shoes.
Take off smile.

The party's over.

Complaint Department

Hello, let me speak to the complaint department.

How is it that I'm being so overcharged in grief? This is excessive, and someone has to do something about it. It's not that I'm unwilling to pay my fair share now—the price for loving and having been loved. But this is too much.

It's not as though my husband and I spent all day, every day together. We said "good-bye, have a good day" in the morning. We said "hello, how was your day" at night.

So why, then, should I have to feel these waves of grief sweeping in at any time of day or night. Sometimes *all* day. Certainly *every* day.

It isn't fair!

We did not share every interest, every activity. He liked concerts of Schoenberg or Bartok, I went to hear Springstein and Diamond. I loved to study languages in depth, he was satisfied to learn a few phrases. Then why is it so many things that interested me then seem so flat now? Why do I now haunt classical music counters at bookstores—and haven't read in Spanish or French for a year?

It isn't fair.

We did not live on a desert island, just the two of us. We had our family, friends, pets. And, thank God, I still do. Then why is it the world seems so deserted now?

It isn't fair.

I did not come into existence, fully grown, when I met him. I had a childhood, education, job, identity—the first part, or opening act, of a life. Then how is it that I feel so rootless and confused about my role now?

It isn't fair.

We did not always agree on everything. We had our own opinions, our own emphases—sometimes emphatically and irritably expressed. Then how is it that I would gladly eat my words by the paragraph *now*, when they seemed so necessary *then*?

O.K., maybe that's fair.

It's not as though I'm trying to weasel out of accountability. I'm certainly willing to pay my fair share. I know there is a price for everything—even loving and being loved. The price of the years of being two, is usually that one is going to be one.

But this bill is too high: all this grief coming at any time for no reason or for all reasons.

I demand a refund. Let me speak to the manager. I
demand some happiness credited to my account,
here and now.

Hello? Hello . . . ?

Operator, I think I've been disconnected.

∞

Tides

∞

Prelude: Once upon a time, many moons ago when we were first dating, we sat together on the rocks of a deserted beach in springtime, watching the moon rise over a lake. The young half moon made a shining path across the water, curving up into the clouds. How romantic it was. "Isn't that beautiful?" I whispered, reaching over to touch your hand. You raised your face to the moonlight, awestruck. "Can you imagine that lopsided little son of a gun up there pulls the tides in and out?" you asked. By the time I stopped laughing, I had fallen in love.

Just when you think the tide of grief
    has subsided a little,
    it comes surging in force.
Just when you think that it has withdrawn
    to a manageable level,
      where you get soaked but won't drown,
    it pours in past the barriers.
Sweeping everything in its path.
Leaving even the high ground wet
    with unshed tears.

But how?

I know that the moon draws the tides
        by the force
        of its gravitational pull,
        as it moves in its orbit
        around the earth.
Distant, sometimes invisible.
But always there.

How it is that such enormous tides of grief
        can be generated
        by someone
        who is absent
Drawn by a void, a space, a hole?
Where is that lopsided son of a gun
        who pulls the tides of grief
        in and out?

Or is there something
        just beyond the horizon
        I cannot see?
Is there something,
        someone
        there?

Identity Crisis

I am feeling more or less like me now.
More or less.

I sound more or less like me now.
More or less.

I suppose it's a good thing to be
　　　the me I remember.
More or less.

But, oh, how that me that was me
　　　misses the you
　　　that was you.

Ordinary Time

The day of the funeral some friends brought flowers to the house with a note: "He is still here. He has not gone far. He's in the next room. The door's ajar." I put the note away then so I wouldn't lose it. I cannot find it. But I could not lose it.

It's been over a year now—the longest year, the hardest year, in some ways the swiftest year of my life. Surely you can't have been gone a year now. A whole year without you?

And yet surely it must have been longer, far longer than that.

Sometimes it seems impossible that you are gone. A bad dream. You are so present—somewhere obscure, but *there*. Just not in any of the rooms I've been in. Nor in any of the rooms I can go in. Yet.

And sometimes it seems a dream that you were ever really here at all. Coming home to you, your coming home to me. All the mundane, interesting, trivial, routine, wonderful things of life.

Did I really live that life once upon ordinary time?
Lucky me.

I have read that it is perfectly normal to feel a certain
envy of couples who still have one another—not a
begrudging, but a wistfulness. But I don't, not now at
least, or rather not in exactly that way.

Oh, I feel envy all right, and why not? If only I could
trade places with her. She had so much happiness.
And quite frankly, I'm not even sure she deserved it.
Certainly she didn't fully appreciate what she had.
Like I would. Now.

Oh, yes, I feel envy. But not of other couples. No.
The one I envy is . . . me-with-you.

∞

Small Sneaky Things

∞

"Memory is the domestic form of time travel."
—Joyce Carol Oates

It is the small sneaky things that get you.

Not the big things that you expect—things like holidays, birthdays, celebrations. Feeling pushed by the obligation to be—or seem—happy. Those can be difficult enough at times, God knows. Remembering how things used to be, could be, should be. And never will be again.

But they have a fixed place, a fixed time, a fixed number. No one has a birthday every day. Some of us don't even admit to having one every year. But the small sneaky things. They can be infinite. Day in. Day out.

With the big things. At least you see them coming. They don't sneak up from behind and yell "Gotcha!"

A blue neon light in a shop window that is the exact color blue of the awnings on a small town restaurant where we had dinner one Saturday night on vacation, our last vacation together. Gotcha!

Lighted windows in other houses when I walk the dog at twilight. Reminders of home the way home once was—the two of us and the children, around the dinner table. Gotcha!

A fragment of music heard on while on telephone hold that teases my memory. Gotcha!

Scraps of paper in your handwriting. Informal reminders to yourself about house repairs, projects and other things to do. Gotcha!

A car horn that sounds like yours when you used to turn into the alley leading to the garage. The sound that meant you were home. Gotcha!

A recipe seen on a box at the supermarket that I might have tried because you might have liked it—or maybe not. Gotcha!

The crisp, cold way the air smells on a moonlit winter night. For no good reason other than because that's the way the air smelled on all those winter nights with you. Gotcha!

Small Sneaky Things. Reminders of past joys, some unrecognized—at least at the time. Small Sneaky Things. Reminders of present pains.

As a child, I learned to say a morning offering to God: "I offer You my prayers, works, joys and sufferings of this day . . . ." I have begun saying it once again on the train on my way to work.

But for all these months the word *joys* has seemed so out of place.

But maybe if Small Sneaky Things can bring pain, they can also bring peace. And, perhaps, sometimes even moments of something close to joy.

Not the type of upspringing, careless joy that comes so effortlessly and unbidden. That was part of us, of the comfort of all those years together—the joy of loving and being loved by someone who could live with you all those years and still love you and find you interesting.

But other moments of *almost* joys:

- Curling up with a cup of tea and a contented cat.
- Dinner with a friend.
- A good book.
- Being able to help someone.
- Having someone willing to help me.
- The first signs of spring.
- Thinking of where you might go for vacation. Yes, *you*.

Maybe it's a matter of taking each moment for what it is now. Not as it was then. Not as I wish it could be. But as it *is*. With whatever joy I can find in this moment.

I know it won't be easy. I would drag back our years together forcibly from the vast storehouse of time if I could.

But if I remember only how different it was *then*, I won't have a *now*.

And so it is that I try to remember to offer my prayers, works, *joys* and sufferings of this day. Even if the joys take some doing.

∽

Saylorville Lake

∽

Somewhere in central Iowa is the farmyard where my uncle, his fiancée, my mother and my aunt used to picnic on a mild summer afternoon. I've never been there, but I can picture it as if I were—the tree-shaded picnic bench, with bowls of potato salad, cole slaw and chicken; the tilled fields across the road, fragrant with the occasional patch of alfalfa, and in the distance the line of trees marking a small woods.

At least that's how I imagine the scene. My uncle, his fiancée and my mother are no longer with us; the only person I know who remembers those picnics is my 92-year-old aunt. And the land where they picnicked is now deep under the waters of Saylorville Lake, the reservoir formed when the Army Corps of Engineers built the Saylor Hydroelectric Project and Dam.

There is something about the whole picture that I find profoundly mysterious, rather magical and a little scary: that a place where my relatives once ate now sits under hundreds of feet of water, forever inaccessible and unseen. The actual site could have been in the shallows, of course. But somehow I see it at the very depths of the lake. And it is this depth and inaccessibility I find so fascinating. Most places you can at least return to, even if they have radically changed. But not if they're at the bottom of a lake.

The days and months and years my husband and I spent together have vanished. They are now flooded by the waters of time, as inaccessible as the picnic area under Saylorville Lake. I can never go back, except in memory and imagination. And yet, those days and months and years were *there*. And my husband lives on, inaccessible for now, but *there*.

Windows

Springtime windows opened to the newly warmed air, the aromas of dinner mingling with the scent of lilacs and coming rain, filling each of us with the indefinable springtime longing that arises from the suspicion that somewhere down some unknown road is the perfect place and time.

Summer windows. The notes of a piano floating through the starched curtains, drifting in the breeze among the leaves. Chopin, I think. A nocturne. Not by an electronically reproduced professional, but by an amateur. A good amateur who might have been you. Who now should be you. Who never again will be you.

Lighted windows in the smoky dusk of an autumn night. The symbol of home. Moving shadows glimpsed behind the blinds. All those years. You, me, the children, a sometime guest. So ordinary. So cosy. So remote.

Winter windows framing a Christmas tree wrapped in light—flickering, flashing, motionless, moving, red, blue, green, gold. It was your job to put up the tree, a job you passed along to your oldest, then to your youngest when the oldest moved on. It was always my job to take the tree down when the holidays were over. The ornaments were still on the piano, waiting to be boxed, when the first of the condolence cards with your name were placed beside them.

Barred windows, to keep the known in and the unknown out.

Opened windows some people lean through to breathe the air, to water a window box, to call a name.

Oh, if there were a window I could lean through, just for a moment, to call your name.

If Only

If only I had known of the silent killer
　　　　stalking your heart,
I would have moved heaven and earth to defeat it.

If only I had known that there would be no
　　　　tomorrow morning,
I would have never left the hospital that night.

If only I had known that an ordinary Saturday in
　　　　January would be your last day on earth,
How carefully I would have held the days before it.

If only I knew then what I know now,
How carefully would I have held all the years before.

If only I could have offered you the choice of being
　　　　the survived or the survivor,
Would it feel less "this can't be" to me now?

If only I had known just how the pain of your loss
　　　　would feel someday,
Would I so happily, heedlessly, have accepted that
　　　　first fateful date?

Yes. Oh, yes.

⌒ᗡ

The Club

⌒ᗡ

Greetings, sisters and brothers. We are members of the most exclusive, inclusive club.

We are old, young. Black, white. Male, female. Gay, straight. We speak every language. We are doctors and carpenters, lawyers and servers, secretaries and writers, bus drivers and teachers, sidewalk artists and chefs. We are rich. We are poor. We are middle class.

Under ordinary circumstances, this might be a rather good club to join. Many of our members are very nice—just the kind of people you'd like to spend time with. (Of course, some are less congenial and some are downright unpleasant.)

But these are no ordinary circumstances. You can't decide you want to belong to the club. The admission is experience—the experience of utter, profoundly painful, take-your-breath-away grief.

Grief makes us members, but it does not—of itself—draw us together. It can just as easily drive us apart. Love and hate, fear and courage—all can be the by-products of grief. But grief is still all-inclusive. It cannot be contained with boundaries, borders or barricades. Grief overwhelms everything in its path.

There are no regular meetings of this club, no minutes, no officers, no subcommittees, no badges or secret handshakes. And yet, by a peculiar grace, we have a special bond that may be acknowledged in a look, a word, a hug.

Once we are initiated into this club, we are forever changed. We can grow, we can shrivel, we can do both at different times. But we cannot remain the same.

So, my brothers and sisters, remember this: You are not alone. We are in this together. We are members of the club. We are those who have known the meaning of loss through love, and of love through loss.

∞

The Last Bridge

∞

The Widow shifted the Day she was carrying and looked around for an empty spot in the small park. But the only space was at one end of a bench next to an elderly woman wrapped in a dark green shawl, her patterned cane propped up next to her. Although the old woman was seen now and then around the village, no one knew her name. Everyone referred to her, respectfully, as the Ancient Crone.

"Do you mind if I sit down?" the Widow asked

"Please do," the Ancient Crone answered. Up close she looked both older and younger than expected, as though time hadn't quite made up its mind.

The Widow nodded her thanks and sat down on the bench to rest, closing her eyes. She didn't know when she had felt so tired. It wasn't just the weight of the Days themselves, however. What was so overwhelming was the thought of carrying all those Years Ahead.

Every morning when she began the Day and every evening when she began the Night, the Widow would ask herself one question: "How am I ever going to carry all these Years Ahead?" Not to mention all the Days, Weeks and Months bundled into all those Years.

111

The odd thing was that she had carried dozens of Years Before, barely noticing their weight. Whole decades had passed in the blink of an eye. An infant grasped the crib bars, said "mama" and "dada" and vaulted into the first grade. A toddler played with a toy piano that turned into a guitar with amps. A second grader set off for the library and returned with high school textbooks. Again and again, Weeks and Months slipped and slid and wiggled with sparkles, stings and surprises.

Then came the Years Before when the Widow was one of two.

"Do be careful, my dear, or you're going to drop it and ruin a perfectly good Day." The Ancient Crone's hand touched her arm gently and pointed to the Day that was slipping from her lap.

"I don't know that I'd call it good, let alone perfect," the Widow replied, rather tartly. By now it was a rather shabby looking Day, a bit frayed here, beginning to fade there, with edges that felt rough and sharp to the touch.

"I understand, dear," the Ancient Crone said. "It looks rather as if you could use a new one."

The Widow, somewhat ashamed of her ungracious tone, said, "I'm sorry. I'm not usually this irritable." She paused. Something about the Ancient Crone invited confidence. "It's just that I'm very tired. It's not just this Day, you see. It is all the Years Ahead. I really don't know how I'm going to manage carrying them." It occurred to the Widow that the Ancient

Crone appeared to have carried considerably more Days than she had.

"But why in the world are you trying to carry them?" the Ancient Crone asked. "Time is not made of pounds or ounces or kilograms, you know."

The Widow glanced at the leaves beginning to rustle above them. Before the Day ended, it was going to rain. Already a mist was forming over the distant hills. "Then what do you think time is?" the Widow asked, because she wanted to know.

"Well, if you remember your elementary physics, I suppose you could say that, technically, it is a measure of motion." The Ancient Crone's tone was mildly reproving. The Widow looked at her sharply. Ancient Crones were an odd lot. "Although that's not exactly what I'd say about time myself."

"And what would you say?" the Widow asked, since that seemed to be the expected question.

The Ancient Crone's eyes were thoughtful behind her squared spectacles. "Bridges. Not just any kind of bridge, but rather a system of bridges—stone bridges growing moss; suspension bridges swaying in the wind, connecting causeways, winding through the middle of things; narrow slippery log bridges like those in the Forest of What Ifs; railway bridges; steel and cable bridges; hidden little footbridges between the banks where flowers grow. Time is bridges all linked together."

"Bridges," the Widow repeated doubtfully. "And where do they all lead?"

"Why to The Last Bridge, of course," the Ancient Crone answered. "And a splendid sparkling bridge it is, its spires like silver arrows pointing through the clouds."

It began to rain lightly and the Ancient Crone got to her feet, leaning on her cane. "And all the discarded Days," she added, "they become part of The Last Bridge. A tiny strand of cable here, a piece of pylon there." She wrapped her shawl about her and with a small wave of farewell started off down the street.

The Widow glanced at the soon-to-be-discarded Day she was holding. If anything, it looked even more frazzled than before. Not a very promising candidate for structural distinction. But the Ancient Crone had been kind, and surely she meant well. The Widow raised her hand to wave in return, but the old woman had disappeared.

Bridges indeed! What a preposterous idea. The Widow picked up her Day and then paused. What was that?

It was only there for a moment—if she had seen it at all.

Just for a moment, just at the corner of her vision, she thought she had seen the flash of a soaring silver spire tip shining through the mist.

Decisions and Dandelions

Like dandelions they sprout—decisions, decisions, decisions. As soon as one is taken care of, another and another spring up to take its place.

Sometimes it seems as if I have had to make more decisions in the months since I became a widow than I ever had to make in a whole lifetime before. Or maybe I just wasn't aware of them as acutely as I am now, when there is no place to dump the decisions I don't care to make.

It's not that I never made decisions before. But then was different. You and I could divide them up, make them together, or toss them back and forth. If we agreed, surely we were right. (Even if occasionally we were wrong.) If we disagreed, at least we had a second opinion. *The* second opinion.

And even then, I had an uncanny ability to unmake up my mind when shopping:

- two trips to exchange a pair of pants

- three to select and exchange a parka

- and once, with assorted friends, six trips to select, exchange and finally reselect a coat.

Yes, I can still get opinions. Solicited and unsolicited. Insightful or not. Welcome or not. But they are not *the* second opinion.

Once, long ago, you told me that I should never ignore my instincts in decision making—that even when I had all the rational information I should still use my intuition, since I made my best decisions that way. And I filed that advice away for future reference—because my instincts told me that you were right. So, maybe you are with me in all this decision making after all.

And so, in the spirit of the Serenity Prayer, I make the decisions that need to be made, delay the decisions that shouldn't be made now, and pray for the wisdom to know the difference. Then I hope they are generally right—or at least not egregiously wrong.

One decision I have confidently made: As soon as the fall sales begin, I am going to donate a certain article of clothing to an appropriate agency and go shopping for its replacement.

I never did like that coat.

ⓥ

Birthday Presence

ⓥ

Today would have been, was, is your birthday.
Never mind the number.

You were so easy to please, but so hard to buy for.
Remember the year you exchanged the special
        Italian hat I gave you for one shirt,
        one belt, and six pairs of socks?

All those years of singing happy birthday to you.
And the songs that were sung to me.
All those wishes for happy returns.
Where are they now?

Yes, once again, it is difficult figuring out
        what to give you.
Knowing that there really is nothing now
        I can give you at all.

Can I give you my love? You already have it—
        well-worn, familiar, still valued,
        but surely nothing new.
Can I give you my prayers? You have them. But
        they're being asked of you as well.
Can I give honor to your memory by trying to live
        life wisely and well? Yes, but that's being
        reshaped day by day.

So what can I give you that you don't have and
        wouldn't return?
I can't think of a thing.
Except perhaps this.
These words are for you,
        and for the others who have gone before,
        like you,
To be remembered by others
        like us.

≈

Beyond the Southern Cross

≈

Stars and sunsets point to something far beyond themselves. They have a poignant beauty that leaves you vaguely dissatisfied as you gaze in wonder.

Now when I look at the skies, I like to think of my husband seeing what I see. But I also try to see with him far beyond the sunset, beyond the stars over my small portion of the Earth.

There are uncounted stars and well-counted constellations I have never seen. Among them the Crux, or Southern Cross, visible only below the 30th parallel.

But it's there. Beyond the curve of the horizon. Beyond my vision. Many others have seen it, perhaps now even him.

Even as I reflect on all this while riding a city bus, however, I see from my window a man who reminds me of my husband, and my vision contracts once again to my little spot in the world—the place where he should be now and is not.

I am not sure what it is I cannot believe: that he is no longer here, or that once upon a time he was well and truly here.

Again I struggle for perspective—of what can and cannot be seen. I try to recall what lies beyond the radiance of the sunsets, beyond the stars, beyond the Southern Cross.

≈

Dream Journey

≈

This was not the first dream I have had of my husband since his death. And I hope it will not be the last. But when I awoke, I knew that it was intended as a conclusion for these reflections, if not for my grief.

Such dreams don't come to me often—with some semblance of plot and filled with symbols. When they do, it's as if my subconscious mind grows tired of sending me unopened messages and says: Look, let me lay it out for you.

We were on vacation together, in some unknown place in some unspecified town in Texas. We had just arrived and were looking for the registration desk. But when I turned around, my husband unexpectedly disappeared. This was surprising, but not alarming, so I began looking for him. After all, he had to be somewhere nearby—he had been there only a moment ago. But the search proved very frustrating. He seemed to have vanished completely.

We must have had reservations. The simplest thing would have been for me to check in, go to our room, and wait for him. But that never occurred to me. It apparently wasn't an option in my dream. So I kept wandering around, searching without success.

Whatever the accommodations, from the outside the resort was not at all prepossessing. The view was nonexistent, consisting largely of a vast empty parking lot. The buildings, such as they were, were oddly clustered, and the closest thing to a pool was a shallow blue stream where a few children played.

It seemed obvious that this was not what we had expected. It would probably be best for us to stay overnight and then check out the next day and go elsewhere. Meanwhile, I decided to look for him at the larger pool I was told was farther on, hoping the resort would look better as I walked. It didn't. We certainly hadn't chosen well when we booked this place.

Oddly enough, the few guests seated at scattered round umbrella tables seemed to be having a fine time. I paused by several tables to ask the people how they liked the place and if they were planning to stay on, and much to my surprise they were. Not a single guest seemed to share my dissatisfaction. It was as if they had a much different perspective on the place than I did, as if what they saw was not at all the same as what I saw.

On and on I walked, looking for my husband; it occurred to me—too late—that we really should have arranged where to meet if we got separated. I was beginning to lose hope that he would even be in the pool building, which was a large boxy brick structure with a few small windows—no wide panoramic poolside views here. It looked more like a Victorian jail. Not only that, it seemed to be at a considerable distance from the lodge where the rooms were. What kind of resort planning was this?

I asked one of the people sitting at still another of those ubiquitous round umbrella tables why the pool building was so far away. They explained that the resort was under construction and would be much different when it was finished.

The more I looked around I saw that the place certainly was unfinished. In fact, the new lodge building they pointed out as under construction in still another parking lot looked more as if it were in the process of falling down. And still the people looked happy and upbeat.

Still, moving on was looking better and better to me. What was most important was to be sure my husband would be pleased with wherever we went. It had dawned on me as I kept on walking that my husband did not have much longer to live. That should have been unspeakably shocking and depressing.

But it wasn't. I was so happy that he was alive *now* that I could think only of *now*.

And then I suddenly woke up, in my room, in my city, in my *now*.

And the remembrance of my undreamed loss flooded in.

There are many possible interpretations of this dream. They are not one-to-one correlations, where this element here stands for that experience there, but several insights seem obvious.

The first is my husband vanishing. In real life, he died so unexpectedly that at times it still seems impossible that he is gone. This impossibility is a root experience for widows—and all who grieve. How often we say to ourselves, "This can't be!"

Next, I am certainly in a place that I don't want to be and don't like. You could also say that my life—a relatively new widow's life—is under construction. Perhaps—one hopes—that it will look better later. But it doesn't seem like a place for lingering now.

Finally, you could interpret the dream to mean that my husband and I do have a room reserved somewhere wonderful and I will be joining him later. Perhaps the resort is another world, another life, where others see things much differently from what I am able to see and are very happy with it.

You could focus on any or all of the above, or find still other meanings I haven't thought of. But this I know:

- I certainly didn't choose to be in the place where I am now—in Never-ever Land.

- Statistically it was likely I would arrive here someday. But *maybe* and *sometime* are not at all the same as *now*.

- Whether I like it or not, I will have to participate

in this resort's construction. Not only to keep it from completely disintegrating but to have some say in its design.

- I have met and will meet people here who can help me and whom I hope I can also help.

There are other things I don't know, but I hope, request or believe:

- that God is with me as I try to find my way around in ways I can't see, don't understand and sometimes doubt.

- that this place is not the last resort but a way station on the journey.

- that there are vast parts of this new place I haven't seen.

I don't know, but I believe, that when I finally reach the registration desk—assuming they honor my reservation—I will see, waiting in the vast and beautiful lobby beyond, those I have loved and lost, especially my husband.

And meanwhile, I hope that the goodness of this man I loved—and the goodness of all those beloved who have gone before us—is being amply rewarded in a place where they can sit at round umbrella tables in the soft sunshine, seeing something wonderful, beautiful, unimaginable

Something I am as yet unable to see.

Other Grief Resources

From Grief to Grace: Images for Overcoming Sadness and Loss by Helen Reichert Lambin. This unique, gentle book addresses the powerful emotions common to all experiences of grief, using images—some religious and some secular—to assist people in naming, processing and overcoming their grief. (96 pages, $8.95)

Hidden Presence: Twelve Blessings That Transformed Sorrow or Loss edited by Gregory F. Augustine Pierce. Real stories by twelve spiritual writers about a tragedy they experienced that led to a real blessing in their lives. Includes "Table for One" by Helen Reichert Lambin. (176 pages, hardcover with gift ribbon, $17.95)

The Death of a Wife: Reflections for a Grieving Husband by Robert L. Vogt. A collection of poignant reflections for any husband mourning the death of his wife. Each of the thirty-one brief stories, remembrances, meditations and poems considers a different facet of the grieving process. (112 pages, $9.95)

The Death of a Parent: Reflections for Adults Mourning the Loss of a Father or Mother by Delle Chatman. This book is filled with stories of people who have lost a parent and how they worked their grief. A spiritual reflection concludes each of the sections. (128 pages, $9.95)

The Death of a Child: Reflections for Grieving Parents by Elaine E. Stillwell. Filled with examples of people who have lost a child and how they dealt with the reality of that event. This collection of life-giving lessons touches on a wide range of emotions and situations that parents may encounter after the death of their child. (160 pages, $9.95)

The New Day Journal: A Journey from Grief to Healing by Sr. Mauryeen O'Brien. Designed to help those mourning the loss of a loved one work their way through the four tasks of grief: accepting the reality of the loss, experiencing the pain of grief, adjusting to change, and creating memories and goals. (96 pages, $9.95)

Available from booksellers or call (800) 397-2282
www.actapublications.com